Copyright / Disclaimer

Table of Contents

About the Author

Alisa Blum began her career as a clinical social worker in 1984. For twelve years she provided individual, family and group psychotherapy, clinical supervision and directed a training program for graduate social work students.

Since 1996, she has provided consulting, training and coaching to businesses and organizations, delivering programs that: enhance employee retention; help employees feel more valued, motivated and productive; enhance teamwork; manage change effectively; decrease stress; resolve conflicts effectively; and help managers develop strategies to work effectively with a multi-generational workforce. Alisa is certified to provide the Social+Emotional Intelligence Profile and provides assessments to help organizations to select top talent. She has worked with city, county, state and federal governmental agencies, non-profits, small businesses, Fortune 500 companies and professional services organizations. Alisa co-authored the book, *Six Word Lessons for Transforming Conflict with Mindfulness,* with Judith Sugg, Ph.D.

Alisa has a Masters Degree in Social Work from The University of Maryland and a Bachelors Degree in Psychology from Towson State University. She has served on the adjunct faculty of Augsburg College, Clark College, Portland Community College and Portland State University.

Introduction

There's no denying the devastating impact that losing a job can bring. Besides the obvious financial stress, unemployment often impacts the way we feel about ourselves. For many of us, the contributions we make from our work build our self-esteem. Work often provides us with a sense of purpose and a social support network. It's no wonder that people who are out of work find themselves feeling despondent and isolated.

Given all of this, maintaining a positive attitude can feel like an oxymoron. I have developed a process, via this workbook, that will help you to combat the tendency for a negative attitude to overtake you. You will find that maintaining a positive attitude not only makes you feel a whole lot better, but will help you get the job you want. Since our attitude shines through when we communicate, maintaining a positive attitude will help you network more effectively, improve your interviewing skills and ultimately, increase the possibility that you will get a job.

This workbook is divided into six areas: *Developing a Positive Vision of the Future, Understanding Where Messages About Ourselves Come From, Changing Your Negative Self-Talk, Leveraging Your Strengths, Seeking Out Positive People, Finding & Providing Inspiration and Taking Care of Yourself.* I have also included some very helpful articles written by colleagues of mine.

There are a variety of ways in which this workbook can be used. It can be used as a self-study guide for the person who is self-motivated and likes to work alone. For those who are more motivated when working with others, I encourage you to gather together a group of people to work on this material with you. If you desire a more structured approach, I provide group and individual coaching. A train-the-trainer program is available for organizations. Contact me at alisalblum@gmail.com for information about coaching and training programs or check out my website at developtopemployees.com.

This workbook is not intended as a substitute for psychotherapy. Please seek professional help if your emotions are interfering with your ability to function.

“Life’s ups and downs provide windows of opportunity to determine your values and goals. Think of using all obstacles as stepping stones to build the life you want.” Marsha Sinetar

Daily Accomplishments

When we are working, we are aware of the tasks we accomplish each day and this sense of accomplishment makes us feel good. When we are unemployed, we are often not only feeling to some extent that we have failed because we have been laid off, but feel like we are not accomplishing as much as when we are working. Therefore, a major component to maintaining a positive attitude is to track your accomplishments.

Make multiple copies of the following page. Keep it with you and note everything you are doing that is moving you toward your goal of getting a job. Your accomplishments can range from getting out of bed in the morning, eating healthy food, and exercising, to tasks that are more traditionally associated with the job search such as attending networking events, sending out your resume and going on job interviews.

Daily Accomplishments Log

Date:

Accomplishments:

1.
2.
3.
4.
5.
6.
7.
8.
9.
10.

Developing a Positive Vision of the Future

There are many people, such as South African President and former political prisoner, Nelson Mandela, and psychologist and Holocaust survivor, Victor Frankl, who survived incredibly adverse conditions because they had a positive vision of the future.

Instead of dwelling on the difficult situation you are in, your attitude will improve tremendously by focusing on your dreams for the future. To do this, get comfortable, close your eyes if you want, and imagine yourself in your ideal work environment. Develop a clear image of where you are working, whom you are working with and what type of work you are doing. Imagine the sights, sounds and smells associated with this vision.

Use the remainder of this page to write or draw your vision of the future.

Vision of the Future

Understanding Where Messages About Yourself Come From

The messages we have internalized from our childhoods have come from a variety of sources such as our families, the media and school. These messages can unconsciously affect how we feel about ourselves. In order to develop a more positive attitude, it is important to become aware of these messages and work on letting go of the negative messages.

Our most powerful messages have come from our **families**. Because our families influence us in our most formative years of development, the messages we receive during childhood can have a major impact on us throughout our lives. For example, if you heard a lot of criticism as a child and internalized these messages, you may be excessively hard on yourself. If you can remember moments when family members expressed pride in your accomplishments, you will start feeling more proud of your accomplishments.

We are living in a **media** saturated culture. The media sends us powerful messages regarding beauty and success and often plays into our culture's gender and racial stereotypes. For example, a former student of mine hung posters of beautiful models in her bedroom because she thought this would inspire her to become more physically fit. This only sabotaged her efforts, because she was holding herself to an impossible standard. When she let go of her desire to look like a model, and became more self-accepting, she became more physically fit.

The messages we received about ourselves in **school** still reverberate as adults. These messages may include whether we are smart enough or too smart; or whether we fit in or not. For example, if you had learning difficulties in school, you may have received negative attention from some of your teachers, causing you to doubt your ability to be successful. You may also have had teachers that were able to see your potential and by focusing on these messages, you will be more likely to feel like you can succeed. Feeling accepted or rejected by peers when we were in school can influence how we feel about ourselves as adults. Try to focus on the messages you received from peers that accepted you, rather than the peers that did not accept you.

Where Do Your Self-Messages Come From?

In each column write the positive and negative messages you have received from your family, the media and school.

	Positive Messages	Negative Messages
Family		
Media		
School		

Beginning today, make a commitment to focus on the positive messages and discount the negative messages!

Changing Your Negative Self Talk

Dr. David Burns popularized the cognitive behavioral approach in overcoming depression and anxiety in his best selling book, the *Feeling Good Handbook*. A central point to this approach is that our thoughts affect our feelings and our feelings affect our behavior. Therefore, if you want to change your behavior you need to first change your thoughts. The way to accomplish this is by changing your self-talk.

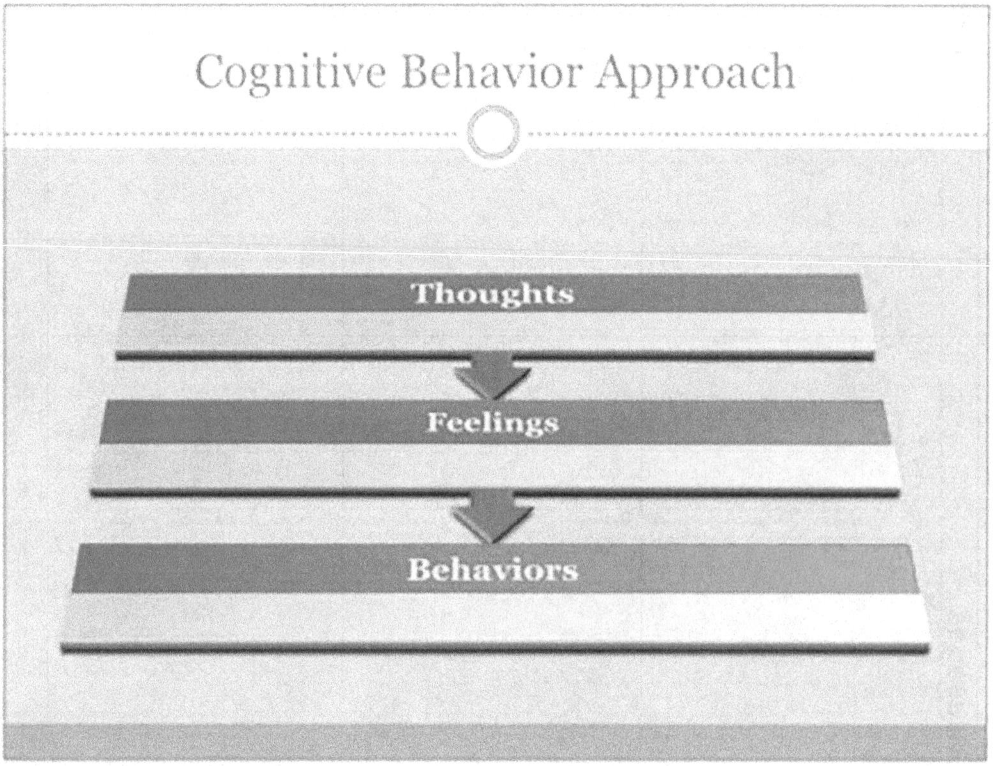

Negative self-talk tends to be instinctive and becomes more pronounced when we are under stress. Therefore, you can expect the negative chatter in your head to increase when you are unemployed.

How often have you found yourself thinking:

- *"The employment situation is so bleak, I'll never get a good job again."*
- *"I've been unemployed for 6 months. I should have a job by now".*
- *"Everyone that I interview with is younger than me. No one wants to hire anyone who is my age".*

To change your negative self-talk you need to consciously develop a more rational response. Here are suggestions for changing the statements above to more rational responses:

- *Each day presents with new job opportunities. My next job may be better than my last.*
- *Because there are so many people looking for jobs, I need to be patient because it may take awhile longer to find a job. I am doing all I can every day to find a job.*
- *I know I'm competing with people who are younger than me. I have to show prospective employers what an advantage it can be to hire someone with my background and experience.*

To begin the process of changing your negative beliefs, you will need to work on countering your negative thoughts with positive thoughts. Use the worksheet on the next page to write down your negative self-talk and counter it with positive self-talk. The more you do this, the more automatic the process will become.

Changing Negative Thoughts to Positive Thoughts Worksheet

Negative Self Talk	Positive Self Talk

Leveraging Your Strengths

The Gallup Organization has done a tremendous amount of research showing that employees are the most successful when their work encompasses their strengths. Identifying and leveraging your strengths will help you realize the vast array of possible jobs you may qualify for and ultimately find a job that is the right fit for you.

What are the specific skills that have given you the most success at work?

Which of these skills have given you the most satisfaction?

What feedback have friends, family and former co-workers given you as to where they see your areas of strength?

Are there hobbies or outside interests you have pursued over the years that could lead to a new career?

Brainstorm all of the possible jobs in which you can demonstrate your strengths.

For insights into your personality type and which types of jobs you may be most suited for, you can take an online assessment at www.keirsey.com. For a comprehensive analysis of your strengths, take the assessment found in the book, Strengths Finder 2.0 by Tom Rath.

Seek Out Positive People

The people we spend time with have a tremendous impact on our ability to maintain a positive attitude. When we are with others who have an optimistic outlook and support our efforts to stay positive, we can easily stay on track. When we are with people who are negative, manipulative and needy, our efforts at staying positive can become derailed in an instant. Keep in mind that positive people will be more likely to help you in your job search where negative people may try to sabotage your efforts or drain your energy. As you interact with people, pay attention to whether you can develop a mutually beneficial relationship.

To evaluate your relationships, ask yourself:

Which of my relationships are affirming and supportive?

How can I show appreciation for the people in my life that are affirming & supportive?

What can I do to create more relationships that are affirming and supportive?

Which relationships I need to let go of?

Finding & Providing Inspiration

Finding Inspiration

Finding inspiring role models from books and the media who have successfully overcome adversity can help to maintain a positive attitude while you are unemployed. Two books that I have found remarkable are *The Last Lecture* by Randy Pausch and *Always Looking Up* by Michael J. Fox. In *The Last Lecture*, Carnegie Melon professor Randy Pauch, views his life events from an incredibly positive framework despite his fatal diagnosis of pancreatic cancer. *Always Looking Up* allows us to see Michael J. Fox's amazing ability to stay positive despite suffering from the increasingly debilitating effects of Parkinson's disease.

Make a list of books or movies that can provide inspiration to you.

____

____

____

____

____

____

____

Make sure you are surrounding yourself with inspirational books, movies, videos or T.V. shows on a daily basis.

Providing Inspiration
Providing inspiration to others will help to keep your attitude in check. This is particularly important if you have children. Since it is rare these days to find a person that has never been unemployed at some point in their lives, you will provide inspiration to your children by teaching them by example, how to cope with unemployment. Additionally, if you have young children at home, you will ease their anxiety if they see that you are coping well.

Ask yourself:

What messages am I providing to others about how I am coping with unemployment, through my verbal and non-verbal behavior?

What can I do differently so that my behavior inspires those around me?

Taking Care of Yourself

Often when you are unemployed you feel like you need to spend every waking hour looking for a job and in doing so, neglect taking care of yourself. People can instinctively tell when a person they are interviewing is under stress. Therefore, if you seem to be under stress while in a job interview, a prospective employer will be less likely to hire you. Focusing on eating healthy, exercising and finding time to relax will actually increase the odds that you will obtain a job.

Check which of the following ways you take care of yourself:

- o Physical Activity
- o Rest
- o Relaxation
- o Healthy Eating
- o Positive Social Contacts

List the activities you can do more of every day to take better care of yourself.

____

____

____

____

____

____

____

____

____

____

The Job Interview:
An Actor's Perspective

By Nancy McDonald

Times are tough, and more and more former employees or freelancers are finding themselves with a feeling of being "back where I started." Here you are again, confronting the Job Interview. "Haven't I paid my dues? Do I still need to do this?"

Well, nobody knows downtime like actors. There is even a special term for it. Rather than being *out of work* or *between jobs*, actors are *resting*. Nice and peaceful, isn't it? But comforting as the term seems, it can actually be an extremely productive time.

The Audition

The interview is your one chance to be "on." They get to see the potential you on the job. Will you be the person that they can trust? Can they rely on your commitment to get the job done? to move seamlessly to become part of the work ensemble? Are you demonstrating those skills now? And how do you "be yourself" anyway? To show the best *you* possible will take some preparation:

1. **Research the company and interviewer.** The more you know, the more ready you are. Check out their company culture so that you can dress and speak appropriately during the interview. You could come off seeming uptight in a relaxed environment or too laid back for a more traditional corporate culture.
2. **Give yourself a mock interview.** If you were the interviewer, what might you ask yourself? Have fun with the role playing. It will help you lighten up and enjoy the real interview. Don't shy away from the tough questions.
3. **Videotape yourself.** Tape your interview answers as though the camera were the interviewer. Evaluate your performance:
   a. Was your voice strong and clear? Did you have a lot of non-words (um, like, uh)
   b. Was your body language strong and controlled (watch for table-rapping, looking away, looking down, nervous movements)

4. **Be ready for your entrance.** Practice entering a room as if you were going from the waiting room into the interview room. Be aware of your breathing. Slow and steady. In your mind, see yourself as "the one." Tell yourself "as soon as they meet me, they will be aware of my strengths immediately. I don't have to *do* anything." It will relax you and your focus can then be on the joy of meeting this person and having a great conversation.
5. **How to stand out.** Use vivid language, action words, words that sell you, strong definitive words (watch out for *sort of*, *if*, *have to*, *hope*, *maybe*, *trying*). Use hand gestures that paint a picture (count off a list, illustrate a point).
6. **Make a strong exit.** Double check with them that you answered all of their questions satisfactorily. Develop your closing line. Make it your own. Something strong and memorable. Even if it's just a thank you. Always use their name: "Thanks so much, Mr. Robinson" or "Thanks for your time, Susan" depending upon your relationship. Practice with your props (gathering your briefcase, purse, coat... make it seamless).
7. **Practice, Practice, Practice**. Be sure you have some privacy. The more you actually physically rehearse your interview, out loud, entering, sitting and exiting, when it's time for the real interview, you will be ready.

Break a leg!

Nancy McDonald's diverse background as an actor, director, producer, corporate trainer, arts educator and private coach has given her a unique perspective and innovative style. Using the discipline of theatre as a foundation, her ability to see the big picture while still being able to focus on details has helped management, employees and staff of numerous organizations bridge gaps and build roadmaps to creative problem-solving. Find out more at www.jugglingfeathers.com.

Positive Self Talk

An excerpt from *Smart Isn't Enough*
By Kenton R. Hill
Management Consultant and Work Performance Coach

Glen Winter, a fifty-two-year-old certified public accountant, found himself overwhelmed by his workload and the mountain of paperwork that had piled up. He needed to develop his self-motivation skills to reclaim his self-respect and to retain his clients.

...Practicing his goal of following his daily plan, coupled with his efforts to temper his perfectionism, helped Glen in his ascent of the mountain of backlogged projects.

Just as Dave, my Mount Hood climbing guide, had from time to time stepped to my side and reminded me to "Keep a steady pace." "Improve the step for the next climber." "Drink plenty of water." "fuel up – eat something." And my favorite, Don't forget to breathe." Positive self-talk reminders like these were part of Glen's development plan as well.

Early mantra-type reminders that helped guide Glen up his mountain include "First things come first." "Being perfect isn't all it's cracked up to be." "Good enough is good enough." But the most powerful was the one he posted in bold letters on the wall, visible each time he looked up from his computer" REMEMBER ROGER WILKINSON!

Glen arrived at this one through his experience of multiple procrastinations. He had picked up this file many, many times in previous months only to put it back on the pile, believing it was "too tough a case" and besides, "Roger is dishonest." But a day came when Glen and Roger's file met up. Is was a day when Glen was sticking to the plan he had committed to in his efforts to catch up. It was the day Roger's file was pulled and placed at the center of Glen's desk. The first item for the next day.

When Glen applied his newly developing discipline to Roger Wilkinson's file, he found to his surprise that it was much easier than he had feared, and also he was able to complete it within his own ethical standards. The project he had stewed about for several months, the file dreaded more than any on the pile, was quickly resolved. By reminding himself to, "Remember Roger Wilkinson!" Glen was becoming his own guide – his own coach. He also added reminders, "I have a plan. I am working my plan. My plan is working."

This technique of positive self-talk, which I originally experienced on my climb of Mount Hood, also proved effective in helping Glen reach his professional development goal of self-motivation. This tool helped him find ways to face and overcome what he had previously labeled the three "P's" of his predicament: procrastination, prioritizing, and perfectionism.

Kenton R. Hill
503-224-1330
ken@kenhillkrh.com
www.smartisntenough.com

Recommended Reading

Bell, Gregg. *Water the Bamboo: Unleashing the Potential of Teams and Individuals.* Portland, OR: Three Star Publishing, 2009.

Burns, David, M.D. *The Feeling Good Handbook.*
New York, NY: Penguin Group, 1999

Fox, Michael J. *Always Looking Up: The Adventures of an Incurable Optimist*. Hyperion, 2009

Hill, Kenton, Phd. *Smart Isn't Enough: How Developing Your Personal Intelligence Can Transform Your Life and Career*. Xlibrus Corporation, 2007.

Pausch, Randy. *The Last Lecture.* Hyperion, 2008.

Rath, Tom & Harter, Jim. *Well Being.* New York, NY: Gallup Press, 2010

Rath, Tom. *Strengths Finder 2.0.* New York, NY: Gallup Press, 2007

Shimoff, Marci. *Happy for No Reason.* New York, NY: Free Press, 2008

Sinek, Simon, Mead David, Docker, Peter. *Find Your Why.*
New York, NY: Penguin, 2017

Sinetar, Marsha. *To Build the Life You Want, Create the Work You Love.* New York, St. Martin's Press, 1995.

CPSIA information can be obtained
at www.ICGtesting.com
Printed in the USA
LVHW061905041220
672996LV00020B/424